TOM HENRICKSEN

The Habits of Great Developers

The little things that can set you apart

This book is dedicated to my family. Jess, Ella, and Matthew: you make life fun!

Contents

Preface

At first, I wasn't sure I was cut out to be a software developer. My initial career transition was from sales. I haven't met many people who have made a similar transition.

I felt like an impostor. Or, as kids used to say, "a poser." (Do kids still say this?) I tend to get in my head and overthink things.

Although a great anecdote to that is action. Once I jumped into my first internship and full-time work, I enjoyed the challenges.

Lost

After almost ten years, I looked up and thought, "Is this all there is?" I felt lost in my work. There wasn't the initial challenge I enjoyed with problems that were fun to fix and with lots of learning along the way.

I thought there was something big missing from my career as a software developer. There wasn't a major triumph that I could think of. I have never had a "singing angels moment."

Consistency

As a voracious reader, I looked for answers. My mother bought my brothers and me a copy of *The Slight Edge: Turning Simple Disciplines Into Massive Success* by Jeff Olson for Christmas.

My mother was an Iowa Hawkeye football season ticket holder. That year the team went 12-0. When the team was asked why, they said the whole team read *The Slight Edge* before the season. For Christmas, she picked up a copy for each of her three boys.

The main takeaway I got from reading this book was the power of consistency. The author went from a beach bum to a top sales representative by applying practices daily. I began to examine my day. Then I applied some of the principles to my career.

Habits

Later, I picked up a copy of *Atomic Habits: An Easy & Proven Way to Build Good Habits & Break Bad Ones* by James Clear. I started to see where many people used daily habits to change their life.

What about software developers, I wondered? Did they have habits they should leverage? I started asking around.

That is how I have come to write this book. My quest was to find the little things that can turn every day into a masterpiece of productivity.

I reached out to many different software development experts. Some I met through hosting online events. Others, I ran into by following their blogs or reading some of their books. Primarily, I reached out to them via email. I am grateful for their responses and advice.

One specific thing I noticed from lots of these experts was to focus on small steps. This helped me immensely. When I initially started development I tried to see the completed process.

Now I just try to look for the next step. Focus on your most pressing issue. Solve it and move on. This one learning gave me confidence and keeps me moving forward.

Acknowledgement

I would like to thank all of the people who have shepherded my career in code. First, at Iowa State University, I had many great professors who taught me the basics. The team at Zirous shared with me the ropes. Without them, I would never have been able to launch my software development career. I have enjoyed their friendship and guidance throughout the years.

1

Starting Your Journey

As you step out into your software development career for the first time, you are optimistic. You see this as a great journey that you are about to embark on. This is probably true.

However, along the way, there are bound to be obstacles. These may include challenges with technology, people, and life.

In my paid internship, I was amazed at the issues that came up. There seemed to be a lot of work for me and the rest of the interns that none of us expected. It appeared we weren't to be trusted with this work.

Contributions

Despite that fact, we sat idle for much of the time. I was essentially relegated to creating spreadsheets of bugs. Although I had found a place to begin, I was underutilized and found myself bored much of the time.

"Wait, I have taken some programming courses! Shouldn't I be writing code?" I thought to myself. I felt that I could contribute so much more, and I was frustrated.

A few months later, I accepted a full-time job. The new organization was a consulting firm. We were expected to have forty billable hours a week.

Solving Problems

The workload was quite different. My colleagues and I were given substantive work to do from day one. We were able to contribute, and we were called upon to solve problems.

I enjoyed that work. It kept me busy and provided me with an opportunity to learn new technology. I would later find out that these two things were important to me.

As I reflected, the two organizations moved at different paces. The smaller company was swifter and nimbler. It wasn't lost on me that the larger company I first worked for found smaller firms like I was part of to help them become productive. The smaller company had focused expertise that the larger did not have. Therefore, this helped me see the value of specialization.

After bouncing around to a few positions I came to a low point in my career. It was about ten years into my career. I had ups and downs. I would enjoy a new job for a while then get restless and move on. By this point, I was in my fifth different job and company.

I thought if only I learned technology X I would be more successful. Then I would get some certification. I still felt inadequate.

Perhaps it wasn't a technology problem after all.

So I began to watch and ask other developers. I was trying to understand why they were successful in their careers.

Company?

Well, maybe I am in the wrong company. Each company and new job started with promise until the reality set in. Different company, the same problems.

Over the years, I kept in touch with Steve. We had worked together a few years earlier. One day, while we were having lunch and explaining my dilemma, he said, "Did you ever think the problem is you?"

Common Denominator

I sat there, stunned. Then Steve continued, "The common denominator in all your issues is you."

After a moment of reflection, I said, "Thanks for the feedback." Although, at that point, I don't think I meant it.

When the mirror of accountability is held up to you, it can be quite difficult. Do we listen or make excuses?

I knew Steve was correct. Of course, I had some defensiveness welling up in me.

2

Engaging the learning process

My mother was a teacher. She always had lots of books in the house. She read to us frequently. Trips to the library were routine in the summer months.

In my adolescent years, I read about sports figures I idolized. Football and basketball greats shared their struggle and success in their autobiographies.

Read

One book my mom had lying around was Stephen Covey's 7 *Habits for Highly Effective People*. I began to read it and enjoyed the advice he shared. It seemed practical and enlightening.

This book was a start for me. It made me realize that I could make changes by using these habits. Success wasn't guaranteed if I followed the advice, but it would help.

Failing

During my high school years and into college, I would occasion-ally use what I had learned. When I stopped, the results ranged from subpar to drastically bad.

For instance, I took a Business Statistics class. I began to neglect the homework. I wasn't being "proactive," to use Covey's term. By the end of the semester, I was failing.

This brought me to academic probation. I had to retake the class and study and plan. I began with the end in mind. I put in the work to pass and get off probation.

Daily Habits

My development career had similar fits and starts. I would learn and then neglect my skills. The result was poor performance and struggle. My mother then bought me the *Slight Edge*, as I discussed in the preface.

The book discusses the daily actions we need to take and compares them to making deposits in the bank. Our careers need them to keep growing.

Adding more items to your to-do list can work up to a point. Today I am going to exercise, do meditation, and read for twenty minutes. With only 24 hours in the day, we have constraints. Review what you already do, and look for ways to remove the negative items.

Schedule Learning

Today, I have learning scheduled into my week. I keep my technical skills sharp. Along with that, I also work on my soft skills, too. Enhancing communication, relationships, and influencing skills helps in any career path.

For example, I am currently studying for an AWS Certification. I use LinkedIn Learning and Udemy courses daily to prepare for this. These are low-cost options to learn and do it consistently. Schedule learning in your work day. Remember your company and career growth depend on it.

What is one skill you could work on daily? How can you schedule that?

3

Stop the Memory Overflow

In college, we nicknamed one of our classmates "Earache." I'll bet you have met someone like this. They tell you about all they know.

He would tell you about current events, his classes, and what foods he liked. Most people would find an excuse to leave his side. "Wow, I need to study for my next final exam...."

Lazy Humans

I recently had an email exchange with Dustin Thostenson. I first met him at Startup Weekend. We have got to know each other through the years. During our conversation, he shared some great insights.

Humans are lazy. Make it easy for them to understand you. Give them the problem and the solution. If they want more details, they will ask. They will be thinking about the details so your answer will make sense.

This reminds me of the basics behind Kanban. It is a simple workflow model that started in manufacturing. Essentially, it is a pull model. Don't push things into the system.

Memory Overflow Error

Then Dustin shared this gem with me.

If you are giving all the details that brought you to your answer, you will lose them. Memory Overflow error.

I spit up my coffee when I heard that one! That is an apt analogy that us technical types can understand. We tend to overshare. Coding can keep our heads in the weeds. Especially if we talk to someone in a different position or level, we need to shape our message.

Analogy: a comparison of two otherwise unlike things based on the resemblance of a particular aspect. From Merriam-Webster.

Dustin's analogy really makes sense to developers. We have seen this before. Of course, we have all used StackOverflow too.

KISS Method

During high school, I had a portly and opinionated Agriculture teacher. He would cover many topics, and he would often pontificate.

Repeatedly, he would tell us to use the KISS method: Keep It Simple Stupid. Don't overcomplicate things.

Developers are guilty of violating that principle. We create detailed processes. Then we code overcomplicated solutions.

One of my co-workers and I created a Help Desk application. We spent weeks designing it and coding it. It had multiple file and bells and whistles.

Then we showed it to the Help Desk team. They shared one

comment: "This looks really nice, but we just needed to help reset customers' passwords."

Wow! we went a little overboard there. Wasting a lot of time for something unnecessary. Asking questions and keeping it simple would have been a better approach.

Design

I recently read *Clean Architecture: A Craftsman's Guide to Software Structure and Design* by Bob C. Martin. In the book, he cautions us about overengineering. "Uncle Bob" shares his disdain for overblown solutions. For example, he details a solution with hundreds of files that essentially copies files which is something we could do with one or two files.

Having worked for an Oracle (a large software company) partner in the past, that hit home. I worked on Oracle SOA projects. We created gargantuan answers to simple questions.

One of our clients was an energy company. We had to pass data about the raw material they consumed. This style of architecture would create, at a minimum, three parts for each action. There were approximately 50 actions. Therefore, we created over 150 files. Many of these were simple actions.

The hardest part of the design is making it just right. It takes a lot of experience to perfect it. So be willing to make some mistakes and learn from them.

Relationships

"No one cares how much you know until they know how much you care" — President Theodore Roosevelt.

Initially, as an introverted developer, I believed the best idea always won. Then I began to notice a pattern. We tend to agree more with people we like.

For instance, Jim and Laura both joined the company at the same time. They had previously worked together.

Working with them both, I saw a great rapport between them. They were clearly friends, but they didn't only say "yes" to each other. They would also challenge one another. For example, Jim would push Laura to expand on her ideas. It looked tense at times, but they knew how to collaborate. Their honest and open approach gave the team an example of powerful cooperation. It made the team better.

Credit

"It is amazing what you can accomplish if you do not care who gets the credit," said Harry Truman.

Great ideas rarely come from one person. As we work together, we help others find solutions. Collaboration is the name of the game.

Improv is a fantastic skill to learn. It is not just for comedians to use. The simple "Yes, and ..." exercise can help us start. Whatever your partner says, you say, "Yes, and ...". A teammate might suggest adding a new screen on an application. You could say, "Yes, and we can display the menu, too." We want to accept all suggestions at this stage. It helps to keep the ideas flowing.

Build on the previous ideas. Don't worry about who gets the credit. Optimization for the team and work completed is the goal.

Wisdom

In college, I took an elective in Philosophy. One definition of philosophy is "a pursuit of wisdom." Working in technology that moves so frenetically, *wisdom can seem elusive.*

Dustin closed our exchange with this. "Just use your over-analytical mind to work through all the details and have the correct, simple answer. " Then he shared this image. It ties this together quite well.

Used by permission. Tom Henricksen. 2023.

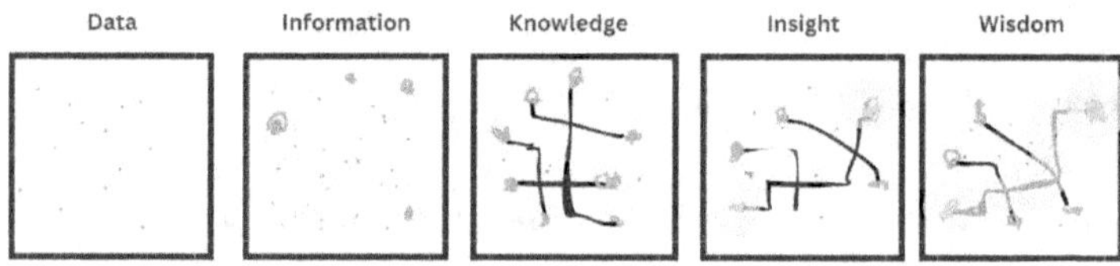

4

Programmers Know the P-Word

I stare at my code editor. The stack trace is quite intimidating. I searched the internet. Nothing.

"This sucks!" I said to my cubicle. Working with proprietary code makes Stackoverflow useless.

I guess I can ask Rhonda. So I do, but then she has to tell me about her cats and garden. Perhaps not...

Give Up

Programming can be a lonely life. We toil away in silence. That can make our minds play tricks on us.

It can be easier to give up than to move forward. Quitting is easy. Full stop.

Hard-Wired for Safety

Our brains are programmed to see threats. Long ago, this would come in handy for our ancestors. They had to beware of the bears or lions.

Today, we imagine more threats than we see in real life. Our lives are much safer overall. Our minds keep going.

There are more things ... likely to frighten us than there are to crush us; we suffer more often in imagination than in reality. —*Seneca*

I recently emailed a former co-worker and friend, Luke Wenz. He is a respected technical leader and developer. Luke always has fascinating insights.

I asked Luke what a good habit was for a programmer to have. He responded with this thought.

I think one of the most important habits a good programmer can have is to be persistent. For example, if you encounter a problem or difficult situation you are able to be resourceful to either find a solution (e.g., online searching, book) or know who to ask to make progress until accomplishing the desired outcome.

I like how Luke goes for the "P" word: persistent! Too many of us are looking for magic answers. He hits the nail on the head. Great developers show up and dig in.

Samantha was an intern that I worked with. She was only a sophomore at the time, so her skills were lacking. Samantha had not taken the courses many of the other interns had.

I could tell she was frustrated with her progress. Summer interns only have a few weeks to contribute to their projects. We spoke about what she was doing to catch up. "I feel like others have more tools than I have."

I shared with her some tips and said I could help her to learn a few things. We went over a few basics, and I could see her pick-up speed. She worked hard that summer and finished the project. Her skills were on the same level as more experienced developers. Her persistence paid off!

Obstacle

I once interviewed Jono Bacon about his book, *People Powered*. In this book, he shares how he created developer communities for many companies. As he was describing his community-building efforts, he mentioned another book. Jono related the story of a friend who had cancer.

He gave this friend a copy of *The Obstacle Is the Way* by Ryan Holiday. Jono said how his friend was helped by it. The book shared some principles to allow them to cope.

I picked up a copy immediately. Holiday does a great job of sharing the many obstacles we encounter and teaching us lessons. As with coding, we have to overcome challenges.

So, as you sit down with your code, remember this one word: persistence. Don't let things distract you. Instead of giving up, keep buggering on!

5

Surprising Developer Habits

What habits do you think developers should focus on? I emailed Tim Andersen, an agile coach and software developer. I met Tim at some Agile Iowa events. Over the years, we have met for lunch and coffee.

Tim's Advice

When I asked him about developer habits, he replied, "Developer habits! There are so many things I could talk about here." He knows the ropes and understands what it takes to succeed in corporate work and consulting.

Hotkeys

Tim reminds us that we need to learn small things and big ideas. "A lot of it has to do with learning or skillset acquisition, but I think there is something more interesting." Productivity and learning go hand in hand.

Autopilot

As a developer myself, I always like to see people leverage their brains. He shares, "I would maybe go a bit deeper and geek out on how to habit-hack your brain. For something to stick, it needs to become automatic." This is comparable to how you wake up the same way every day.

Hack Your Habits

Tim shares how he learned to hack his habits. Through reading books like *Atomic Habits* by James Clear and *Tiny Habits* by BF Fogg, Ph.D., he saw what was possible.

"Each habit has a queue, craving, response, and reward. By reverse-engineering the process of how something becomes a habit, we can be more intentional about the habits we design."

As a programmer, this is right up our alley. Essentially, we can tap into the Human API, which is a way to interact with people. *Think of this like a cron job for people.* While a cron job is a scheduled task for your computer, a habit is a routine you do at a set time. This gets my mind racing with opportunities.

Writing

The last piece of advice that Tim shared surprised me. I am guessing it may surprise you, too. It is something that we do often, but it is frequently overlooked.

Writing to a broad group (an audience, or a blog) is incredibly intimidating and difficult to get started with. Writing to an individual, I find, I can do fairly easily.

Developers think of writing code. They are not writing to

communicate. Then many of us wonder why we never can convince others through our writing.

Good writing can influence others. Along with that, it can help us work through our thoughts. Instead of just going into your boss and telling them we need to change something, take a step back and write it up.

Thoughts untangle themselves over lips and through pencil tips —Dr. Howard Hendricks

What are the main points? Create an outline and write up what you want to say. Think about the objections you might get. It can save you a ton of embarrassment. For instance, if you understand common objections, you can address them. If you don't, people will stop reading.

Josh was our business stakeholder. I shared with him how we should change the registration process to use new technology. He couldn't have cared less.

The next time I created an outline for the change, I wrote up what I would say. I framed it from his perspective. I shared how the changes that I proposed would make it easier for users and save the company money. That sounded like music to his ears.

Programmers are like everyone. They have habits, too. We need to leverage our brains' tendencies. Use habits to our advantage and make our lives easier. *Coding can be simple when you use the right habits!*

6

Legendary Developer

I'll bet it is hard to be a legendary developer, right? I asked a legend, Dave Farley, co-author of the best-selling book *Continuous Delivery: Reliable Software Releases Through Build, Test, and Deployment Automation*. What he would say. His email reply had some habits that were much easier than I anticipated.

Dave and I got to know each other as part of my DevOps Online Summit. He was always willing to share his expertise. Dave's easygoing demeanor is part of why his YouTube channel has over one hundred and eighty thousand subscribers!

Keep Learning

Dave started by pointing out that we should always keep learning. Good developers don't just learn one thing and stop. They look for new skills to master. They examine existing skills and find ways to enhance their existing skills.

Find the Best Solution

He also pointed out how the best developers want the best solution—which may not be their own.

The really good ones are not precious about their solution; they are open to it being criticized—they may not always like it, but they want to know how to do better.

Whereas some people only fall in love with their ideas, great developers know they don't have the market cornered.

Understand the Problem

Stop me if you have ever done this. You see an issue and instantly know what the problem is. Then you apply the fix. As you do this you think to yourself, "I don't need to test this."

You tell the QA team it is fixed and move on. A while later, you get an IM, "Hey, that defect you said was fixed is still occurring." Ugh...

Dave reminded me to always work to understand the problem. The better developers among us would try to do this. Don't just jump in and fix it. Step back and ask questions.

Open to Feedback

Perhaps you are one of those people who is good at listening to feedback. I can get defensive. One of Dave's recommendations is to be open to feedback. This way, we can learn from other's perspectives.

We were getting close to completing the project. Krishna, the tester, asked me to please test my fix again. It didn't appear to be working. "It works fine on my machine!" I said and left the conference room.

Rajeev, the project manager, came to talk with me. "Tom, we know this is getting stressful." He paused, then continued, "Krishna is very thorough. Please listen to him; perhaps you forgot something."

I went back to work with Krishna. Turns out, he was right. Feedback can be hard to listen to, but it helps us grow and learn.

Sense of Design

Design can be nebulous. For instance, Tom B was a UI Designer I worked with. He could craft an intuitive interface. I was always amazed at that.

Learning design has been a trial-and-error endeavor for me. I have created applications and refactored them. Dave reminds us to learn and be curious about design.

I think that the good programmers I have worked with have a strong sense of design, which includes always wanting to learn about, and having a very strong understanding of, the problem domain that they work in.

Question our assumptions often. Ask our stakeholders to verify our work. Seek clarity in our design.

Small Steps

I recently listened to the audio book, *The Power of Habit*, by Charles Duhigg. He discusses how organizations can change with small wins. These little steps build momentum. Dave shares this tidbit that helps developers build momentum, too.

The other thing is that they make progress in small steps, evolving their understanding and design over time.

Our best work evolves. It takes steps to get there. Some steps we take are not in the right direction, and that is okay.

22

7

Avoid the Error Conditions

"I'm sailing! I'm sailing! I sail! I'm sailiiiiiing!" said Bob Wiley.

This is from "What about Bob," a movie from 1991. Bill Murray does a great job playing the deranged Bob. After his exclamation on sailing, he reveals his secret.

"My secret is I let the boat do all the work."

As developers, we also have a secret. Our code does all the work. Before we send our code on its way, though, we need to put it through its paces and test it from all different angles.

Test One Thing at a Time

Kanban is a popular workflow management method. One of the strengths of Kanban is its ability to get people to focus. We try to reduce work in making progress—no more spinning plates.

Nick Hodges, an experienced developer and writer, reminds us how this applies to developers. For instance, your testing might be trying to cover five cases at once. That is a sign we need to shift our testing.

You should be able to take your unit test executable and run it on your mother's computer when it isn't even connected to the internet.

Our unit tests should be focused on one thing. That 5-in-1 tool that is in your garage does five things poorly. Unit tests should be a one-hit wonder.

User-Centric

"Next Friday, we are going to the call center to talk to our users." Nakia shared this at our stand-up. I thought to myself, "What a waste of time…." I felt sure that we had better things to do.

On Friday, we began meeting with the call center people. We listened to the live calls they took. At first, I couldn't believe how much information they had to look up. Our application only had a fraction of what they needed.

I learned, that day, the value of our users. Good testing and design are user-centric. Nakia's idea shifted our team. We went from resenting our users to empathizing with them.

Testing took on new meaning. Our exception-and-error handling took a step forward. *We now had a name and a face of a person we knew was counting on us.*

Error Scenarios

Elias Karthan has had a long, storied career in technology. He is the chief operating officer at Zirous, a software company in the Midwest. When I asked Elias about programmer habits, he said this.

As far as good programmer habits go, I think it's essential to think through error scenarios when developing. Often people focus on the happy path and tend to overlook how to handle all the different types of errors best. I think this is especially important when developing integrations when the end-to-end process crosses multiple systems and business processes.

His answer speaks of hard-earned wisdom. Like many of us who have been bitten by improper testing, Elias reminds us to be more thorough.

So, before your code sails out into the world, make sure it's ready. Test it first, one feature at a time. Make sure it fits the user's perspective. Review the error scenarios. Test the complete end-to-end process.

8

Take a Day Off

Real developers never take a vacation! We code all of the time....

Perhaps you have heard advice like this. Or maybe you have worked at a company that implies it.

Choose Wisely

Be careful who you listen to for advice. Look for someone who has had some long-term success, not a flash in the pan.

Bruce Tate, an author and developer, is someone I have followed for many years. I first saw him talk at *No Fluff Just Stuff*. This is a developer conference. After that, I read some of his books.

For this reason, I emailed him for advice for developers. He offered three wonderful suggestions.

Take enough vacation, including all the time off that is offered. Too many of us don't take good care of ourselves, and it shows up later in the form of burnout.

Are you getting close to burnout? Have you taken a break from work? It could be as simple as going for a walk outside.

Like hitting the restart button on your computer, taking a break from work makes things function better. A few days away can refresh your mind. Then you are ready to come back to your work.

Protect the Asset

In *Essentialism, The Disciplined Pursuit of Less,* Greg McKeown shares the importance of rest. He shares how numerous people have thought they could get away with less sleep and rest. Greg calls this "protecting the asset." Of course, that asset is us. Our bodies and minds need rest.

Be Curious

Novelty is a great way to find new foods and experiences. A few years ago, we were in Washington, DC. Our family tried Ethiopian food. It was quite interesting. Eating a new type of food helped make our trip memorable, and the experience has stayed with us. Likewise, as developers, we need to try new technologies and techniques.

Developers need to learn new tips and techniques. This can keep us fresh and give us a new perspective. Bruce had this to say about learning.

Learn new languages and frameworks outside of those you usually use. You'll be surprised how often this can happen on your employer's time. Good employers want to see their talent develop.

He brings up a good point on how this benefits you and your employer. You might find new ways to solve problems. Similarly, develop new skills, too. This is a real win-win.

Compassion

This one is particularly difficult for me. I can get irritable when working on challenging tasks. Patience can be in short supply.

My former boss and friend, Mike Freed, used to call this Irritable Programmer Syndrome or IPS for short. We get deep into work and put on our headphones. Then someone bothers us. We can react quite gruffly. A little compassion goes a long way.

Bruce's last tidbit was this: "Treat others with respect and kindness." This sounds like something we should have learned in kindergarten, although we all may need a periodic reminder.

To summarize Bruce Tate's advice: Make sure you take time off to refresh. Learn new languages and frameworks. See what others are doing. Take this learning back to your current job. It benefits your employer as well as you.

Finally, treat others with compassion. Don't talk down to non-technical people. Meet them where they are, and be patient.

9

The Curious Developer

Are you an apathetic developer? The business people don't know what they are talking about. I have this all figured out.

Arlo Belshee, a lead developer who specializes in legacy code, recently shared some advice via email. The overall theme was to be curious, which is the opposite of being apathetic.

Talk Less

He started with wisdom that I could see Mr. Miyagi giving Daniel in "Karate Kid," where Mr. Miyagi dispensed terse wisdom along with menial work.

Talk less. Listen with open curiosity more.

This short dictum echoes Robert Greene's *48 Laws of Power*. This book distills thousands of years of philosophy into 48 laws. Law 4 is, "Always say less than necessary." Too often, we want to talk a lot, and we say nothing.

Levels of Developer

Arlo takes this deeper. He breaks it down for each role.

Junior Developer

As we start, we need a basic understanding. Ask why the old system weirdly does that thing. Could it use a new tool?

These questions can give you a foundational understanding. Develop interest in the details. This will pay dividends as you go.

Mid-Level Developer

From there, you can begin to see things from the customers' perspective. Why do they have this particular requirement? What makes this the best way to work?

Arlo's questions here give us tools to pry into the customers' minds. Begin to build empathy for the user. See how things look from their perspective.

Senior Developer

Now use your experience to focus on the team. Why did the team react this way to the change? Are we pushing too hard?

Competent coders know they are part of the team. We have to look at everyone in total. Who needs to step up? Do I need to step back?

This also applies to technology. Although you may be quite accomplished, others should have ideas and input. Don't stifle the team.

In the Code

Arlo shared some guidance with different types of code.

Legacy

He handed us this gem for existing code.

When encountering legacy code, be curious about what edge cases and unexpected situations led to the tangled code in front of you. What non-obvious, critical wisdom does it contain?

This reminds me of one of the first applications I worked on. A senior programmer warned me: don't touch this file. It is a mess of spaghetti code. Unfortunately, I had to work on that file repeatedly. I made sure to test and make changes extensively. At first, I was confused, but then I slowly came to understand it.

New

Arlo gave us two questions for developing new code.

1. What does the customer know about their situation that I do not?
2. How can I change my products to meet their goals rather than expecting the reverse?

Answering these two questions can help us glean a better understanding of the customer. They can lead us to do the necessary prodding to get all of the basics down.

Final Considerations

Arlo added these additional thoughts.

What are my blind spots and who can see them? What am I doing that blocks my co-workers from telling me? Perhaps try pair programming. Which is where you pair up and work together. Or better yet you could try mob programming. This is like pairing but includes a larger group collaborating on the solution. These techniques help reveal solutions we won't see by working alone.

When you feel like you have it mastered, ask yourself another question. *How can you and your team move past the question of who is right and towards achieving success together?*

Considering all of this, Arlo has a lot of wisdom. Essentially, we need to be curious developers. We need to ask more questions and talk less.

Think about what role we play. Ask the right questions to bring about success. Find people to collaborate with.

Keep looking for your blind spots. Pair and mob to gain a broader understanding.

10

The Developer Doctor Is In!

When you feel sick call, the Doctor!
  When your code is sick call, Doc Norton!

Doctor Who?

Doc Norton has been helping developers for many years. Through his speaking and consulting, he builds their technical skills. Doc's focus is on things like Test Driven Development (TDD). He puts people at ease quickly.

Doc also helps teams deliver. He is the author of *Escape Velocity*. It helps teams focus on the right things. We met as part of my virtual event, Agile Online Summit.

Doc's Tips

Here are a few tips he shared via email.

TDD

Doc is a big fan of TDD. He finds it quite valuable. It helps teams deliver quality.

Refactor

Refactoring goes hand-in-hand with TDD. As you test, you find improvements.

One personal warning. Don't attempt to refactor without unit tests. It doesn't end well! The first time I heard about refactoring, I thought the unit test were optional. I worked for two days on changing our codebase. Then I deployed it to the test environment. I have never seen more defects in my life! We finally had to roll all the changes back. Next time, I set up the unit test before I refactored.

Pomodoro

The Pomodoro technique is setting 25 minutes to do focused work. Then you take a break. After that, you can repeat.

Doc recommends that we do this to help us focus. I have also found this to be quite helpful. Make sure to mute or close other distractions during this time.

Doc's Habits

When I asked Doc about developer habits, he listed these.

Simple and Small

Create simple things in small steps. Don't get fancy. Take one step instead of a giant leap.

Composition

Be meticulous about composition. This is a design technique for software development. Look at each object that you have added. Does it make sense?

I struggle with this one. This is where I like to leverage Doc's first habit. Ask someone.

Validate

Validate before, during, and after. Don't just test it once. Things change. Mistakes happen.

See Doc's first tip. This aligns well with TDD. Ensure quality throughout the process.

Problem

Know the problem you are solving. Define the main goal from the outset. Make sure everyone agrees.

The stakeholders want a solution. Most often, they don't care how it happens. Solve the problem, and move on.

Release

Release ridiculously often. If you release it monthly, then try to release it twice a month.

Look for techniques to enable this. Perhaps you need feature flags or trunk-based development. The bottom line is: release more often.

Automation

Automation over documentation. I tend to agree with Doc on this one. However, my Business Analyst friends may disagree.

Documentation gets out of date quickly, whereas if something is automated, it works. Reading about something is lovely. Having it work is even better.

On the whole, Doc reminds developers of the basics. Mastery comes from understanding and applying them. Doc is a treasure. We need to listen to him.

11

The Creative and Funny Reverent Geek Weighs in on Developer Habits

What is made of bacon, draws funny pictures, and creates dad joke memes?

The Reverent Geek, of course!

Used by permission. David Neal. 2023.

David Neal, aka the Reverent Geek, is a creative and funny developer. He is an artist and a musician, too. We met as part of my virtual event Agile Online Summit.

I recently emailed him to ask about good programmer habits. His reply focused on these.

Patience

He started with this. "I think a good habit for anyone that is frequently faced with the challenge of learning something new is to have a healthy dose of patience." Did you think of Guns and Roses, too?

He continued, "Give yourself time, and forgive yourself when things aren't progressing as quickly as you hoped." I feel like he has seen me get frustrated.

We want to fix the code right away. Of course, it doesn't always work that way. Take your time, and do it right.

New Job

David Neal_uses the example of a new job. "We often underestimate how long it will take to adjust to a new role before we 'feel productive.'" Slow down, and learn how things work.

The journey of a thousand miles begins with a single step — Lao Tzu

His advice reminds me of the Zen Buddhist concept of the Beginner's Mind, dropping our expectations and preconceived ideas about something. Think of it like a reset button on your computer. Forget all of your preconceived notions.

A new job can be a reset moment. Be mindful of the bad habits you may have picked up along the way. Reflect on how you do things.

Practice

Skills take practice. We need to hone our skills often. David said we need "little steps of regular practice." Build it into your daily routine.

"Practice makes perfect. After a long time of practicing, our work will become natural, skillful, swift, and steady."

· *Bruce Lee*

One great suggestion is the Code Kata. They are programming exercises that help programmers improve their skills through practice. Like learning how to play guitar, it takes practice.

Determination

Software development can be a challenging endeavor. There can be days you want to give up. David reminds us to keep our "determination to stick with it."

Look Back

He closes with this advice. "One day, you'll look back and be amazed at how far you've come." As someone who is prone to action, that made me think.

How often do you think about your progress? Perhaps you are even a new developer. You have taken a few steps. Appreciate what you have learned.

Or maybe you are further along in your journey. The experience you have is valuable. Don't underestimate that. Consider all that you have gleaned over the lines of code.

Be Vulnerable

David has previously shared this post on his blog. He does a great job of modeling vulnerability which is something that is in short supply in the developer world.

Used by permission. David Neal. 2023.

My biggest mistakes had nothing to do with programming.
The most difficult parts of any job, and the most valuable activities of any job, have nothing at all to do with technology.
It's people. How we value ourselves. How we value others.
I couldn't agree more!

Ultimately, David is a wonderful example for us all. He shares his expertise with conference talks, blog posts, and his artwork, too.

He started with this sentence, and I will end with it. *We all need to practice patience.* With ourselves and others. Enjoy your career as a software developer. In closing, don't take yourself too seriously.

12

Daily Deliberate Practice

What if I told you that the little things matter?

For instance, great developers are like athletes. They get their daily practice.

Deliberate Practice

Anders Ericsson is credited with discovering *deliberate practice* which is, *"The individualized training activities specially designed by a coach or teacher to improve specific aspects of an individual's performance through repetition and successive refinement."*

Angela Duckworth outlines this in her book, *Grit: The Power of Passion and Perseverance.* She summarizes it by saying it starts with a stretch goal. We focus on the goal and get feedback on our performance. We refine the practice accordingly.

Developer Practice

So how does this relate to developers? We need to set aside time daily to hone our skills. As Jeff Langr, software consultant and writer, said, "Find[ing] time daily to sharpen your tools, particularly the use of IDE and keyboard shortcuts, command-line tools, vim, etc., much like a professional carpenter or the like might do." He shared this when I emailed him for his suggestions on habits.

Scheduling time is the first step. As Angela points out, we need to add to that. Just putting in the time doesn't do it. Here are a few additional components.

Stretch Goal

What would challenge you? Perhaps learning a new framework or reviewing something you already know. Is there a test you could study for?

A few years ago, I was chosen to teach a Java course to some mainframe developers. I had already been programming Java for many years. Teaching something, though, requires another level of mastery.

Feedback

It can be hard to hear feedback sometimes. The quote, "In writing you must kill all your darlings," has been attributed to William Faulkner. The same thing about killing all your darlings can be said of software.

We need to seek feedback. Our idea may not be as good as we think it is. As with pair programming, two heads are better than one.

Look for two things in your feedback: timely and actionable. After a feature has been shipped is not the time for feedback.

Actionable feedback can be applied where general feedback doesn't help. Don't use "Good job." Instead, use "Remember a String is immutable in Java, try a StringBuilder instead."

Coaching

We need to seek out coaching from more experienced developers. As a neophyte to Vue.js, I have been working with an experienced front-end developer. He has shared many tips with me.

The learning is intense at the start. Then you begin to pick up small lessons here and there. Keep learning. Don't let your skills plateau.

High Standards

In *Grit*, Angela closes by sharing the importance of our team. To become good, we must work with others who are as well. *Find a team of developers who have high standards.*

As humans, we can let things slide, from time to time. If you are in a group that pushes you to get better and learn, you can go farther.

Grateful

We should also remember to be grateful for the work we do. Each day, developers help companies solve problems. Find a bigger purpose in your work.

For instance, I currently work for a health insurance company.

My work helps people live better lives. There is more to what we do than writing code. *See the larger picture.*

In conclusion, take time each day to practice your craft. Set a goal and get feedback. Ask others for coaching and advice. Have high standards for your work. Be grateful for the work you get to do.

13

Coding With Ron Jeffries

Are big leaps dangerous?

They can be.

Ron Jeffries is the founder of Extreme Programming. He has seen many fads come and go in his long career. When I emailed him about developer habits, he had an astounding answer. I met Ron as part of a panel on Extreme Programming.

Small Steps

He shared, "A habit that I'm trying to improve is GeePaw Hills 'Make Many More Much Smaller Steps.' I've found that, while I think I do pretty well at taking tiny steps, he takes much smaller ones than I do."

I tend to be more like a whirling dervish. I code a bunch. Then I am flabbergasted that nothing works. Facepalm.

Ron and GeePaw's advice is tough for me. As I tried it, I found out that it was a refreshing change. It made development more enjoyable.

Limits

Ron continued, "I'm trying to push that limit. I see no downside to incredibly tiny steps." Yes, I would agree.

An additional benefit for me was that it created focus. Limiting our work in progress reduces distractions and blurred thoughts.

Downside

Would there be any issues with this? Ron shared, "I see no downside to incredibly tiny steps." In our fast-paced world, *this is counter-intuitive.*

We want to rush from task to task. Our focus is on completing more work. In *Leadership Is Language*, David Marquet talks about red work and blue work. Red work is doing. Blue work is thinking.

Marquet shares how knowledge workers must do both. You must take time to reflect on your work. How can we improve?

Slower?

He mentioned this, though. "It feels slow but I suspect it isn't, since mistakes increase faster than linearly and are harder to find, as step size increases."

We often speak of speed and velocity. Ron's suggestions to slow down are more holistic. Instead of rushing the coding and creating defects, we take our time.

Coder Flow

In closing, Ron shared this. "I try to Zen through it and keep my voice mellow and low." However, many thoughts keep coming when we need to slow down.

Perhaps this would induce coder flow which is the concept that Mihaly Csikszentmihalyi discovered. He recognized and named the psychological concept of "flow," a highly focused mental state conducive to productivity.

Software development can become flow-like when *we make big strides by taking small steps.* From great minds like Ron and GeePaw, we learn: to try, each day, to achieve coder flow.

14

By George, I Think He's Got It

Details can be my undoing.

    Rushing through a user story. Scanning a blog post. Committing my changes to GitHub. Moving on...

    Wait, is that a defect assigned to me?

Pay Attention

When I emailed software development leader Geoge Dinwiddie about programmer habits, he said, "Pay attention to the details."

    Has he been watching me? Wow! How did he know that?

    My approach has been, *"details, schmetails...."* Of course, that led to a few defects.

    George is right. We need to pay attention to details. Don't rely on automated testing and Quality Assurance to save you.

Question Your Assumptions

If you ever validate an input field, you must be careful. We assume people would only put numbers in the zip code field. A wily-testing veteran schooled me on this. Thanks, Miki. :)

Another aspect is security. Things like Cross Sight Scripting attacks are pretty common. Your validation should withstand that as well.

Question Your Habits

What are your daily habits? Are they serving you? As a big fan of Michael Hyatt's productivity suggestions, I use the Workday Startup and Shutdown.

In Michael's book *Free to Focus*, he outlines these. Essentially, they bookend your day. Akin to what a computer does on startup, the Workday Startup ensures we start on purpose.

George is asking us to audit our programming habits. Michael Hyatt agrees with this practice. We need to periodically ask if this habit helping.

Question Your Mistakes

Steve McConnell points out in his book, *Code Complete*, "We need to learn the types of mistakes we make."

Early in my Java career, I made the same mistake time and again. I would forget to initialize my variables. My co-worker, Ken, would laugh when he saw this repeated error.

State Machine

George also shared, *"Consider a state machine to keep system responses decoupled and easy to modify."* Some practical design advice.

First, you may ask, what is a state machine? According to National Instruments, "A state machine is a programming architecture that allows dynamic flow to states depending on values from previous states or user inputs."

Developers can wrestle with coupling items. Working on early internet applications this was a problem. A hack was to pass a lot of data around to emulate the state.

George shared some direct advice with us. First, he reminded us to pay attention to details. Understand them. See how this can shape our solution.

Then we need to question our assumptions. Ask your stake-holders to see theirs. Create alignment on them.

Third, question your habits. Do you need another round of testing? Or maybe the issue is you don't understand the use case. Could you review it with the product owner?

Additionally, where do you usually make mistakes? As a novice Vue.js developer, I don't understand a few things. Pairing with my co-worker, Ryan, helps me see solutions to my newbie errors.

Finally, George gave us the advice to keep things decoupled. We can use a state machine in our design. This is simple and elegant advice from a software sage.

15

Tips from Otter

"Tiny Bubbles" was made famous by Don Ho. The Hawaiian crooner shared this song at every concert.

GeePaw Hill, a software development coach, recommends coders take small steps. The Agile Otter, Tim Ottinger, a software developer and author, changes it to tiny steps. Tim and Don Ho both like to keep things tiny. Where the tiny bubbles in the wine made Don Ho smile, Tim smiles when developers take tiny steps.

Tiny Steps

Tim concurs with GeePaw. He wants us to work on tiny steps. Go small, or go home!

Shrink down our developer ambitions. Fix one small thing at a time. Ensure it works. Then take another tiny step.

Self-Observation

Take time throughout your day to observe your work. Is it easy? Maybe it is too challenging. Look for ways to change your approach.

Is it too complicated? Perhaps it is time to scrap your design. Start fresh.

Beware of the sunk cost fallacy. Just because you have put in a few hours doesn't mean you can't switch directions.

Curiosity

Curiosity is required for a development career. Tim said, "Take a moment to figure out how something works, or a better way of doing it." Question the process. Then look for improvements.

He added, "Don't settle for a super-shallow understanding of the stack." Sure, we can use something with cursory knowledge. But dig deeper to develop mastery.

Teaming

The idea that developers can work as individuals is largely a myth. Great software is built in teams. Tim reminds us we should be "working in an ensemble."

Additionally, the software is quite complex. So most systems are too much for one brain to hold and manipulate. Pair up, and do your thing. Or get crazy, and Mob.

Test-Drive

Of course, with a nickname like "Agile Otter," Tim is going to have an experimental mindset. Tim states we should be "test-driving changes." Look at the feedback and adjust.

So what do you want to kick the tires on? Create a small experiment. Collect some data. Repeat. Let the learning begin.

16

Do You Do This First?

Isn't being a good developer hard?

Allen Holub, a computer scientist and prolific author, shared some simple suggestions.

I have interviewed Allen a few times as the founder of the Agile Online Summit. He always has provocative opinions.

I emailed Allen for advice for developers. Here are his simple gems.

Write the Tests

Firstly, Allen shared this nugget. *"Write the tests before you write the code, and test every minute or two as you work."*

In *Dream Big*, Bob Goff speaks about mountain climbing. He shares a story of always being close to the mountain with ropes. Bob kept climbing without tying in. Fortunately, he realized that before it was too late.

Allen's advice of testing often keeps us tied in. We are never too far from working code.

Talk to Your Users

Developers are cynical about their users. Earlier in my career, I could put off their requests.

Then I worked with Nakia. She knew our customers. To help us develop empathy for them, she had us take a field trip to their office. We spent a day watching them work.

That day was quite an eye-opening one. We learned how little our application did to help them.

Allen implores us, "Talk to your actual users, ideally as you're working, not after you've 'finished.'"

Get feedback early and often, not once the work is shippable. Allen and Nakia agree. The users can guide you best.

Write the Simplest Thing

Software architecture can become quite stilted—exercises in futility. It pays to be a bit more pragmatic.

The last Allen-ism was this. *"Write the simplest thing you can to solve the problem at hand, not one semicolon more."*

Start with a simple approach. Then add complexity if you absolutely need it. Don't get too cute.

In conclusion, Allen shared three concise recommendations for the coders out there. I enjoy the simplicity of his advice.

Just to quickly recap:

- Write the test first
- Talk to your users
- Write the simplest thing first

17

Collaborate and Reflect

"Developers are all introverts. There is no way to get them to work together."

This is still a popular belief.

Yes, developers can be shy. There are ways to get them to come out of their shell, though.

Woody Zuill is best known for Mob Programming which is complementary to pair programming with more people. He created this with a team he led. Woody has shared this with many organizations ever since. He travels to speak about Mob Programming

When I asked him about developer habits, he began with collaboration.

Collaboration

I'd say my most useful programming habit is to collaborate and to become a collaboration expert. Become a team member everyone wishes to be working with.

This is not a surprise to those who know Woody. He is a gentle guide who helps teams work together.

Part of the success of Mob Programming can be attributed to his kind demeanor. *He is the Mister Rogers of Programmers."*

Safety

Part of good collaboration is safety—psychological safety, to be exact. This is a big topic. Here is a nice definition from the Center for Creative Leadership.

Psychological safety is the belief that you won't be punished or humiliated for speaking up with ideas, questions, concerns, or mistakes.

Many teams create norms to facilitate safety. For instance, they spell out how they would handle conflict.

Take some time to foster a safe environment. Your team will be enhanced.

Team Player

In Patrick Lencioni's book, *The Ideal Team Player,* he outlines three virtues. They are humble, smart, and hungry.

A humble person is a person who focuses on the team instead of themselves.

In this case, smart refers to working with people. That means having a high Emotional Intelligence or EQ.

Hungry people want to learn more and give more.

These are the types of people Woody wants to work with rather than people who only care about their contribution.

Retrospect

Working on agile teams has taught me the importance of reflection—taking a pause or asking how it is going. Like the retrospective helps a team reflect, Woody asks us to do the same.

The second is to do frequent retrospectives (at least daily). In my daily retrospectives, I focus on "turning up the good." We ask: What went well today, and how can we get more of that tomorrow? Literally, how can we get more of that the very next day?

Don't rush to the next day until you learn the lessons from today. My son's basketball coach is fond of saying, "Don't lose the game and the lesson." We don't want history to repeat itself.

Turn It Up

When Woody says to turn up the good, he wants to amplify the learning. As teams discover how to work together, they accelerate delivery.

Think of ways to amplify your teams' greatness. Help them do more. Perhaps that might be removing roadblocks. For instance, your team might need approval to change the way they work.

Reflect

Making time for team reflection in a retrospective is helpful. Do the same on an individual level, too. Consider your level of collaboration.

"All men's miseries derive from not being able to sit in a quiet room alone." — Blaise Pascal

I find journaling helpful for this. Take time and run through some journaling prompts.

Woody's advice is timeless. Teams need to focus on collaboration. That is the secret sauce of groups.

Turn up the good on your team. Periodically inspect with a retrospective. Use the typical reflection questions. What is working? What isn't working? What new things can we try? Your team will thank you!

18

Chris Teaches the C-Word

Great comedy has some truth to it. That is why Nick Burns, Your Company's Computer Guy is funny! This "Saturday Night Live" bit was a mainstay for Jimmy Fallon.

Yes, we developers struggle with communication. Whenever I stumble upon people who are trying to help, I rejoice.

I found Chris Laffra's subsequent book refreshing. Chris is a senior developer and was frustrated with developers' communication skills. So he wrote *Communication for Engineers* to give us a framework to relate information better. His book is available on Gumroad.

Communication for Engineers

He gets the issue. We do struggle with communication.

I like how he says it here:

A rule of thumb to use is to assume that your impact as an engineer is made up of 30% raw coding output, 50% of you talking about your work, and 20% being nice to other people.

Too many of us overlook this simple fact. Our career is not all coding. There is much more.

Compliments

Chris shares the importance of compliments. They help boost others' confidence.

Introverted developers can neglect these subtleties. Small things like this build relationships.

Productivity

We solve coding challenges. It helps if we do it in a timely fashion.

Don't be the flaky developer who is never finished. That will drive your team nuts.

Communication

Chris calls communication the impact multiplier. I love that!

It multiplies your impact.

The reason is that communication is the key to personal success in organizations consisting of more than a handful of people.

I couldn't agree more. Too many coders ignore communication.

Then they wonder why their career suffers. It is all connected.

Ground Rules

Chris shares some ground rules for communication.

1. Just the facts. Share the facts only.

2. Be specific. Share with conviction and tell us what you need.
3. Transparent. Indicate why you choose that option.
4. Consistent. Be clear and concise.
5. Direction. Have a road map to show the way.

These five ground rules help us communicate effectively.

The first one is tough for me. Facts are important.

I would share a caveat. It depends on the type of person you are dealing with.

Humans Are NOT Computers

Developers can assume that everyone is like them. The truth is they are not.

That is why I recommend one step before following Chris's ground rules.

Assess

What type of person are you talking to? For instance, software engineers might focus on technology. Make that assessment.

A few years ago, I tried to make a case for a change to my manager. I detailed the facts of our application.

He looked at me and then told me about the costs. I realized quickly that I didn't speak his language. Costs led him to his decision.

Tools

A good developer knows their tools. As a Java developer, I know my IDE.

When we assess people, we need to do the same. There are many tools you could learn to use. Pick one and know how to use it.

For instance, let's use DISC Assessments. Here are the four types of people.

Dominance: If you meet this type of person, they are results driven. They don't like small talk.

Influence: These people place importance on relationships. They tend to talk a lot about themselves.

Steadiness: These people will want to cooperate. They won't rock the boat.

Conscientiousness: They will want exact details on your expectations. Then they will ask more questions. For them, there can never be too much detail!

If you have talked to someone for more than five minutes, you should be able to tell which type of person it is.

Also, as coders, we can fall into the latter two categories. If your manager is in the Dominance category, they might have trouble talking with you.

Whereas you might need more detail, they can get frustrated. Calibrate your answers to their questions. *What are they looking for?*

Overall, Chris has wonderful advice. Software engineers need a lot of help communicating. We struggle with it, by and large. Use his rock-solid advice.

Make sure to understand your audience.

- What style of person are you dealing with?
- How can I best craft the message for them?

Answer those questions, and you can be more effective in your communication.

19

You Can't Really Code Until You Can Explain It

My development career has allowed me to have many interactions with authors and thought leaders. A few years ago, as founder of the Agile Online Summit, I met Andrew Stellman.

He is an accomplished programmer and author. He has written numerous books for O'Reilly. I asked him how writing helped his software development skills.

Connect the Dots

Writing books on C# helped me become a better developer, and writing books on Agile did the same for helping with projects. A lot of people say that you don't understand something until you have to explain it, and I think there's a lot of truth in that. I think writing about topics helps me connect a lot of dots.

I agree with Andrew. As I develop each day, the writing helps me process the lessons. At the moment, we may want to get our work done. When we create content, we need to make it coherent. We must reflect and connect.

Engage the Reader

Andrew had some additional advice to engage the reader. It helps to have empathy for your reader. Or, as AJ Harper says in her book *Write a Must-Read*, "We need to identify our ideal reader. When we do that, we can capture their attention."

I think trying to write in a way that's easy to understand and engaging helps me a lot. The two books I always recommend to people who want to write technical books are non-technical. The first is the one I already mentioned, "On Writing: A Memoir of the Craft" by Stephen King. The other is "Save the Cat" by Blake Snyder. It's a book on screenwriting, but there are a lot of lessons that we can learn about keeping people engaged and giving them a story.

Even hardcore developers know the importance of a story. Pick your favorite movie, and it's the story that draws us in. In Dan and Chip Heath's book, *Made to Stick*, they remind us that stories are remembered whereas facts are forgotten.

Marathon, Not a Sprint

I grew up watching Chia pet commercials. A Chia pet is the pottery that you can smear grass seeds on. The grass grew quickly in the commercial. It gave us the illusion that it would grow quickly. Growing grass or a team takes time. Andrew outlined some similarities between starting a team with good habits.

Sometimes, I have to remind myself that writing is a marathon, not a sprint. There are a lot of parallels to getting an agile team up and running. A lot of teams will start doing great practices like daily standups, retrospectives, or refactoring, but after a little while those new practices trail off. But if you can get the team to develop real, lasting habits, that's how you get things to stick.

Our daily practices determine the team's health. If we don't have a stand-up and align, we get off track. Andrew has a beautiful combination of technical chops and an understanding of group development.

Technical practices of refactoring code help teams deliver quality code. Too many people don't see that connection. Andrew knows it because he has lived it.

Good Narrative

Greg Jensen, an experienced technology leader, and I presented together at *Iowa Code Camp* a few years ago. His advice to developers is to craft a career narrative. I took this presentation and created *Tech Survival 101*, an eBook available on Amazon. Andrew shares similar advice with us as we code a solution.

Coming up with a really good narrative that explains why—not just how—technology or tools or techniques forces me to understand whatever I'm writing about on an even deeper level.

One thing I have been trying to create a good narrative for is technical debt. As developers, we may see the rotting code even if we don't communicate the severity well to the business. The idea of technical debt, the implied cost incurred when businesses do not fix problems that will affect them in the future, can be hard to make clear to stakeholders.

So what narrative are you going to try to change? Try out a few options, and see what resonates. That is the way to truly understand. Find your people, and engage with them.

Let's review all of the great advice from Andrew. He shared how developers should write to connect the dots. We can see the big picture and understand the moving parts.

We need to engage the reader. Consider who you are talking to. Are you talking to your manager, another developer, or some stakeholders? Focus on good practices for the long term.

Lastly, Andrew wants us to craft a good narrative. This can be more persuasive than just relating facts. Take us on a journey and draw us in. Then we can support you and your work.

20

Direction From Daniel

My mom was driving my little brother, John, and me to the state fair. We were running late. Then we saw a sign that said, "State Fair next Right."

John was sitting in the front seat. He said, "Pat, take the next right."

She responded, "I know a shortcut." Then she turned the car to the left.

Thirty minutes later, we were still lost. No state fair was in sight.

As developers, we need to stop and ask for direction, too. We might be heading the wrong way. Someone else can provide some perspective.

I emailed a few thought leaders in the development space. Daniel Moka from "Craft Better Software" replied with some guidance. I have been following his blog for quite a while.

Baby Steps

In the film "What about Bob," Dr. Leo Marvin shares with the main character, Bob, his advice to use baby steps. Perhaps we developers aren't as neurotic as Bob Wiley, but that advice can be quite helpful, anyway.

Daniel has similar advice for us as we code.

"Taking baby steps and verifying each step. I always work in small [steps], and then I verify each step. By doing so I can prevent expensive mistakes."

These small experiments can yield us confidence and results. It gives us feedback that we are on the right track or that we need to course-correct.

Boy Scout Rule

In high school, my group of friends would camp out on the weekends. We would leave a mess until Mike came with us. Mike was an Eagle Scout. He made sure we followed the advice of Robert Stephenson Smyth Baden-Powell, the First Chief Scout of the worldwide Scout Movement: "Try and leave this world a little better than you found it."

For developers, Daniel says it this way:

"Following the boy scout rule: always leaving the code a better place behind. It also related to practicing continuous refactoring."

In my years of coding, I have seen some gnarly code. Look for ways to clean things up. Delete some dead code that is unused or commented out.

Why Are We Doing This?

In 2009, Simon Sinek published a book that reminded leaders to share the why. In *Start With Why*, he reminds us to think about why we are doing this.

Developers need to understand this, too. Daniel also echoes Simon's advice for coding.

"Always asking the why: Every action we do should have clear reasonings, potentially considering the trade-offs."

It is important to consider the trade-offs. Too often, we overlook the options. For instance, the other day, I was discussing the priority of work with the Product Owner.

Review your code

If you are like me, you get pulled in many directions: meetings of different sorts, and coding when you can. This can create mistakes and defects.

Daniel suggests reviewing our code at every possible opportunity. Here are some of his suggestions:

- Before Git commit
- Before creating a Pull Request
- In the refactoring phase of TDD (Test Driven Development)
- During pair and mob programming session

Find those moments to look with new eyes on your code. As a writer, I know there is creative time and critical time. Editing takes a particular frame of mind. Take a break, and come back to it.

Attention to Detail

Lastly, Daniel advises us to pay attention to detail.

"High Attention to detail: It is the hallmark of software craftsmanship, I believe. I try to care about every small detail of the app, also if it is just a variable name, I name it with care. Things can add up easily."

Essentially, we need to take pride in our work. We need to do it well and look for any small improvements to make.

Daniel Moka shared some great directions to improve our software development: Take small steps. Leave the codebase better than you found it. Understand the why. Review your code. Finally, pay attention to the details.

21

Ask More Questions

Camping can be fun. It can feel good to be out in the wilderness, with fresh air in the morning and the quiet solitude of waking up with the birds.

As we explore the outdoors, we need to leave the campground better than we found it. Luca Rossi recommends we do the same with our code. I consider his Refactoring blog a must-read. When I emailed him, he shared similar advice to Daniel Moka.

Leave the Code Better

When you touch some code, look for ways to clean it up. Refactor the design to make it easier to read.

Don't leave a mess for others. A co-worker of mine once printed out a long method. He hung it outside his cube. It was a mess that many people had touched. It only takes a little time to tidy things up.

Small Pull Requests

Working in Scrum we have short sprints. A two-week time block to complete our work. They give us a timeline to complete our work. Another tip from Luca is to create small pull requests. Analogous to small focused time blocks to work.

Commit Frequently

I am old enough to remember when we had to save our work. In college, I typed a few pages in the computer lab. Then the power went out, and my work was lost.

Luca suggests we commit frequently. I agree, as our code repository can help us track our changes. For example, I may try a few different changes, then I want to go back to an earlier version.

Pair Up

When my daughter was in kindergarten, her class took a field trip to the Science center. Each kid had a buddy to stay with the whole day. As the only father in the class, I had to take ten boys to the bathroom. I was a traffic cop, keeping them together.

Pair programming is one of Luca's favorite ways to work. The extra set of eyes helps spot bugs, along with keeping us on track. We spend less time on social media or looking for music to listen to. Buddies work for field trips and coding, too!

Take a Break

After working from home for a few years now, I realize I can't sit very long. When I have a long meeting, I use my standing desk, or I even walk around my office.

Luca proposes we take frequent breaks to avoid tunnel vision. Getting away from the code can help us clear our heads. We can see new possible solutions. Bruce Tate had related advice.

Ask, Ask, Ask

Luca's last bit of advice is to ask a lot of questions. He wants us to talk to the project managers and stakeholders. We need to understand what they need.

What great tidbits from Luca. As you visit a codebase, leave it better than you found it. Create small pull requests, and commit frequently.

22

The Developer Checklist

Errors in programming can be disastrous.

My computer science professor relayed a story about telecommunications. A developer forgot the semicolon on his program. This brought down the phone system.

Medical errors can be deadly.

In 2009, Atul Gawande published *The Checklist Manifesto*. As a surgeon, he wanted to curtail medical errors.

He shares many tales of people who die or are hurt because of medical errors. Gawande writes about how professionals deal with complex responsibilities.

Checklist Manifesto

He shares how we need to categorize our errors. In the first category, we have errors of ignorance. Essentially, we don't know enough information.

Secondly, we have errors of ineptitude. In this type, we don't use the information we do know. This is the focus of his book.

Common Mistakes

For surgeons, there are common mistakes. Developers make common mistakes as well. What are some of yours?

I tend to rush too much. I want to get my code deployed and overlook some testing scenarios.

Brainstorm Issues

Bring the team in on this. Brainstorm common issues. Perhaps there are a few typical defects. What can be done to fix them?

Scrum teams could add the checklist to their definitions of "ready" and "done."

For instance, a few teams I have worked with pulled in incomplete stories. The velocity of the team suffered as a result.

Higher Standard

Establish a higher standard of work. For Gawande, he wanted to raise the level of medical care.

As developers, we can raise the level of quality. We can reduce random errors by checking common issues.

Short and Clear

Create your checklist to be short, clear, and focused on the essentials. Make it easy to do.

Long and wordy ones won't be used.

Did I create a unit test? Yes, that was easy.

Did I create a unit test that covers all paths of execution, including checking for unused objects? The first time you are rushed, you will pass on doing this.

Create With the Team

I mentioned before that you should include the team in your checklist. This can be a wonderful collaborative affair.

You could gather the developers and get their input. They may have things they check as well.

Similarly, if you include the Quality Assurance team, they will know your tendencies. I forgot to check out-of-state users. Add them to your list.

Revisit Often

Once you've created a developer checklist, make sure to update it from time to time.

As I mentioned before, I created one when I was a beginner Java developer. Now, as I learn Vue.js, I have other items that I focus on. I added them to my checklist.

So keep adding and taking items off your list. Keep it short and succinct. People who create long lists hardly ever use them.

23

Applying the Habits

We are all a work in progress. This book can help you if you let it. I have found wisdom in many other developers' words.

If you have made it this far, something must be resonating with you. Find something small that you can build on.

"Big doors swing on little hinges." — Clement Stone

For me, I know that daily work can bring change. It must be consistent and applied.

We are fortunate to be working in technology at this time. Things are changing fast, but we are ready for it.

Failure

It's Friday morning. I walk into the office and sit down at my desk. My boss, Scott, stops by and says, "Tom, can I talk with you?"

"Sure," I say. Then I follow him to his office.

When he gets outside of his office, he takes a right turn instead.

My mind begins racing. "What is going on?" I ask myself.

Then he takes a left turn into Sandee's office. She is the Director of Human Resources.

As it turns out, this is my last day at that company. I am crushed. I think of myself as a failure.

Growth

A few years later, I picked up the book, *Mindset: The New Psychology of Success* by Carroll Dweck. Carroll shares the principles of the Growth Mindset where we look at our skills not as fixed but as changeable.

This helped me reframe my career journey. Getting fired was feedback. I needed to learn to lead and communicate better.

Progress

Each step along the way was progress toward rebuilding my career. I soon found a job after I was let go. I began managing a team at a small company. Along with those responsibilities, I did software development, too.

Our career path isn't always straight up. Sometimes, it's more of a jagged line of starts and stops. Missteps and learning happen at all parts of the journey. In our social media world, we can compare ourselves to highlight the reels of others.

"Scars are medals branded on the flesh, and your enemies will be frightened by them because they are proof of your long experience of battle."

— Paulo Coelho

Don't hide your mistakes. They will reveal you are authentic. Plus, as Patrick Lencioni discusses in *The 5 Dysfunctions of a Team*, they encourage others to trust you.

It seems counterintuitive, but when we appear vulnerable, people tend to trust us more. I used to think I had to appear perfect. Of course, we all know that no one is. Some of us just don't want to admit it.

You can have a great career as a developer. However, you must realize failure and growth are part of the process. Keep pushing through to find the best spot for you.

Remember that there is not one way to be successful. You will need to work on what that looks like for you. While some may aspire to be a leader, I find success in coding each day. Or perhaps you think the best path for you could be as a software architect.

I realized I don't care to be in that many meetings. Success for me is working alone or in small groups.

Define what success is for you. Live the long game and play it well. Examine life and ask good questions. Without it, you will never know.

About the Author

Tom Henricksen is a problem-solving technology professional. He is a speaker and writer at Code is Easy. Starting from a developer he has worked as a Project Manager, Technical Lead, Scrum Master, and Manager of Software Development.

Tom has helped organizations with agile transformations. He has also coached and trained teams and individuals.

Tom has been an entrepreneur as well. He speaks and writes with a focus on technology roles. Tom was the founder of the Agile Online Summit and DevOps Online Summit. Where he led a strong online community of over 5,000 people.

Tom has learned how to solve challenging issues in technology and lead technical teams. He can help you develop those skills too!

You can connect with me on:

🌐 https://codeiseasy.co

🐦 https://twitter.com/TomHenricksen

🔗 https://www.linkedin.com/in/tomhenricksen

Subscribe to my newsletter:

✉ https://t.co/NkolrQgXHM

www.ingramcontent.com/pod-product-compliance
Lightning Source LLC
Chambersburg PA
CBHW071351130726
47996CB00002B/888